Shuffle Shuffle Rhyme Chime

Contents

Indian Chant Bill Martin, Jr	Page	2
Five Fat Fleas Dennis Lee	Page	4
Before I Count Fifteen Michael Rosen	Page	6
Moonlight Magic Stephanie Wade	Page	10
A Baby Sardine Spike Milligan	Page	12
Sh! Sh! Baby's Sleeping Carolyn Graham	Page	13
Jingle Jangle Chant Bill Martin, Jr	Page	14
Wobble Gobble Michael Rosen	Page	16
The Pickety Fence David McCord	Page	18
On the Ning Nang Nong Spike Milligan	Page	19
Think That's Bad Luck? Kate Lovett	Page	20
Warning Carolyn Graham	Page	22
The Meeting Schoolyard rhyme	Page	24

Rhymes to Read Together

beat upon the tomtom
peat upon the drum
beat upon the tomtom
beat upon the drum
huffle to the right⊳
huffle to the right⊳
peat upon the tomtom
beat upon the drum

3

FIVE FAT FLEAS

Five fat fleas
Upon a trapeze
Did somersaults one by one.
A flea flew, a flea flew,
A flea flew, a flea flew,
A flea flew
and then there were none.

Four fat frogs
On tumbledown logs
Did somersaults one by one.
A frog flew, a frog flew,
A frog flew, a frog flew,
(*Clap*) and then there were none.

Three fat cats
On calico mats
Did somersaults one by one.
A cat flew, a cat flew,
A cat flew, (*clap*),
(*Clap*) and then there were none.

Two fat ants
In dancing pants
Did somersaults one by one.
An ant flew, an ant flew,
(*Clap*), (*clap*),
(*Clap*) and then there were none.

One fat bee
On a billygoat's knee
Did somersaults one by one.
A bee flew, (*clap*),
(*Clap*), (*clap*),
(*Clap*) and then there were none.

No fat gnomes
On a dinosaur's bones
Did somersaults none by none.
(*Clap*), (*clap*),
(*Clap*), (*clap*),
(*Clap*) and then there were none.

One fat bee
On a billygoat's knee
Did somersaults one by one.
A bee flew, (*clap*),
(*Clap*), (*clap*),
(*Clap*) and then there were none.

Two fat ants
In dancing pants
Did somersaults one by one.
An ant flew, an ant flew,
(*Clap*), (*clap*),
(*Clap*) and then there were none.

(etc.)

Dennis Lee

BEFORE I COUNT FIFTEEN

If you don't put your shoes on before I count fifteen
then we won't go to the woods to climb the chestnut tree.
One.
> But I can't find them.

Two.
> I can't

They're under the sofa. Three.
> No . . . O yes.

Four Five Six.
> Stop–they've got knots they've got knots.

You should untie the laces when you take your shoes off.
Seven.
> Will you do one shoe while I do the other then?

Eight. But that would be cheating . . .
> Please.

All right.
> It always . . .

6

Nine.

It always sticks–I'll use my teeth.

Ten.

It won't It won't . . . It has – look.

Eleven.

I'm not wearing any socks.

Twelve.

Stop counting stop counting.

Mom where are my socks mom?

They're in your shoes. Where you left them.

I didn't.

Thirteen.

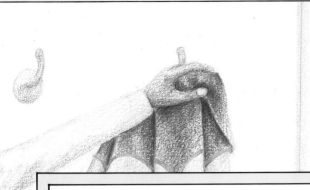

O they're inside out and upside down and
bundled up.

Fourteen.

Have you done the knot on the shoe you were . . .

Yes. Put it on the right foot.

But socks don't have right and wrong foot.

The shoes, silly . . . Fourteen and a half.

I am I am. Wait.

Don't go to the woods without me.

Look that's one shoe already.

Fourteen and threequarters.

There!

You haven't tied the bows yet.

We could do them on the way there?

No we won't. Fourteen and seven eighths.

Help me then –

You know I'm not fast at bows.

Fourteen and fifteen sixteeeenths.

A single bow is all right, isn't it?

Fifteen. We're off.

See I did it.

Didn't I?

Michael Rosen

9

Down down down a little
Hush a little, shush a little
Snuggling, cuddling
Moonlight, magic
Shuffle to the left
Shuffle Shuffle Shuffle Shuffl
Snuggling, cuddling
Moonlight, magic

Slide down here.
sandman's near.
do not peep.
softness, **sleep.**
Shuffle to the **right**
Shuffle to the **right**
do not peep.
softness, **sleep.**

A BABY SARDINE

A baby sardine
Saw her first submarine;
She was scared
and watched through a peephole.

"Oh, come, come, come,"
Said the sardine's mom,
"It's only a tin full of people."

Spike Milligan

SH! SH! BABY'S SLEEPING

I said, Sh! Sh! Baby's sleeping!
I said, Sh! Sh! Baby's sleeping!

What did you say?
What did you say?

I said, Hush! Hush! Baby's sleeping!
I said, Hush! Hush! Baby's sleeping!

What did you say?
What did you say?

I said, Please be quiet, Baby's sleeping!
I said, Please be quiet, Baby's sleeping!

What did you say?
What did you say?

I said, Shut up! Shut up! Baby's sleeping!
I said, Shut up! Shut up! Baby's sleeping!

WAAAAAAAAAAAAAAAAAAAAAAAAAAAAAAAA

Not any more.

Carolyn Graham

Tingle Tangle Tingle Tangl

Tingle Tangle Tingle Tangle

Tingle Tangle Tingle Tangl

Tingle Tangle Tingle Jangle

Shuffle to the lefl

Shuffle Shuffle Shuffle Shuffl

Tingle Tangle Tingle Tangl

Tingle Tangle Tingle Tangle

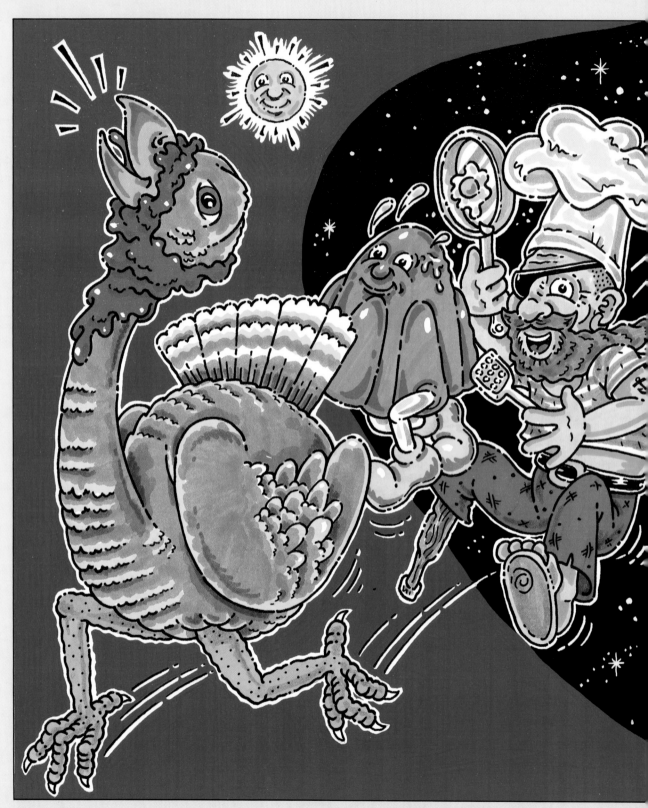

WOBBLE GOBBLE

It was a stormy night
one Christmas day
as they fell awake
on the Santa Fe

Gobbly-gobbler
gobbled Wobbly
Hobbly-hobbler
Gobbled Gobbly.

Turkey, jelly
and the ship's old cook
all jumped out
of a recipe book

Gobble gobbled
Hobble's Wobble
Hobble gobbled
gobbled Wobble.

The jelly wobbled
the turkey gobbled
and after them both
the old cook hobbled

gobble gobble
wobble wobble
hobble gobble
wobble gobble

Gobbler gobbled
Hobbler's Wobbler.
Hobbler gobbled
Wobbler's Gobbler.

Michael Rosen

17

THE PICKETY FENCE

The pickety fence
The pickety fence
Give it a lick it's
The pickety fence
Give it a lick it's
A clickety fence
Give it a lick it's
a lickety fence.
Give it a lick
Give it a lick
Give it a lick
With a rickety stick
Pickety
Pickety
Pickety
Pick.

David McCord

ON THE NING NANG NONG

On the Ning Nang Nong
Where the Cows go Bong!
And the Monkeys all say Boo!
There's a Nong Nang Ning
Where the trees go Ping!
And the tea pots Jibber Jabber Joo.
On the Nong Ning Nang
All the mice go Clang!
And you just can't catch 'em when they do!
So it's Ning Nang Nong!
Cows go Bong!
Nong Nang Ning!
Trees go Ping!
Nong Ning Nang!
The mice go Clang!
What a noisy place to belong,
Is the Ning Nang Ning Nang Nong!!

Spike Milligan

Under the LADDER
Crash goes the MIRROR
Think that's bad LUCK?
Who cares? You care

Shuffle to the left
Shuffle Shuffle Shuffle Shuff

Think that's bad LUCK?
Who cares? You care

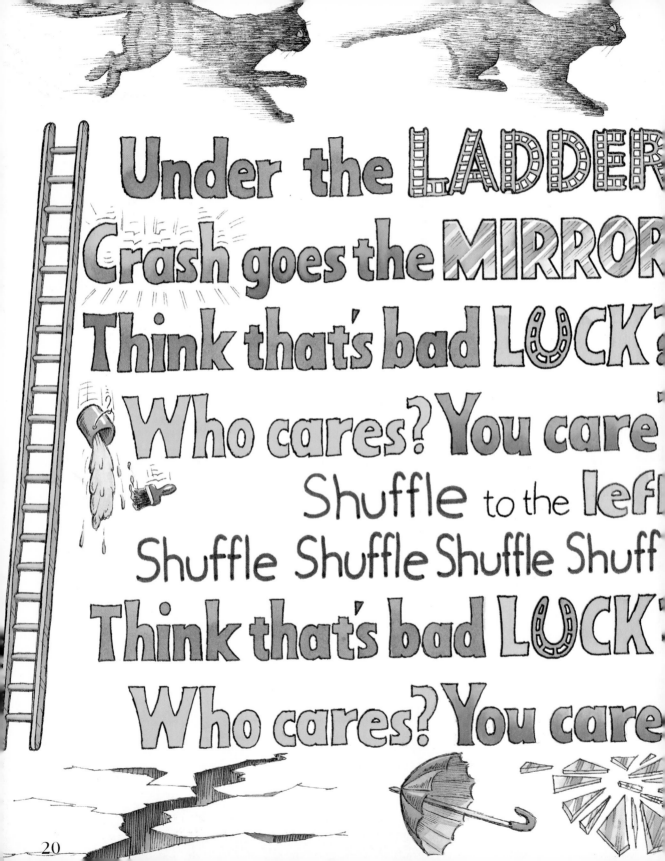

here's a **Black Cat.**

FRIDAY 13

step on a **CRACK.**

Wait and see.

Hey, not me!

Shuffle to the **right** ▷
Shuffle to the **right** ▷

Wait and see.

Hey, not me!

13

21

WARNING

Watch out! Watch out!
Watch out! Watch out!
Watch out!
There's a hole in the floor!
What?
A hole.   Where?
In the floor.
A hole in the floor?
Yes, a hole in the floor,
A great big hole in the floor.
Well, I don't see
any hole in the floor.
I don't see any hole.
It's there!   Where?
Right there!   Right here?
Yes, right there.   Are you sure?
Sure, I'm sure.
It's big as a house.   Big?
It's huge.   Huge?
It's huge.
A huge hole, a great big hole,
a great big hole in the floor.
I think you're kidding.
You're teasing me.
There's no hole in the . . .

Carolyn Graham

THE MEETING

Ladles and jellyspoons,
I come before you to stand behind you,
To tell you something I know nothing about.
On Monday, which is Thanksgiving,
There will be a mothers' meeting
   for fathers only.
Admission is free,
You pay at the door.
Bring your own seats,
We'll sit on the floor.

Schoolyard rhyme